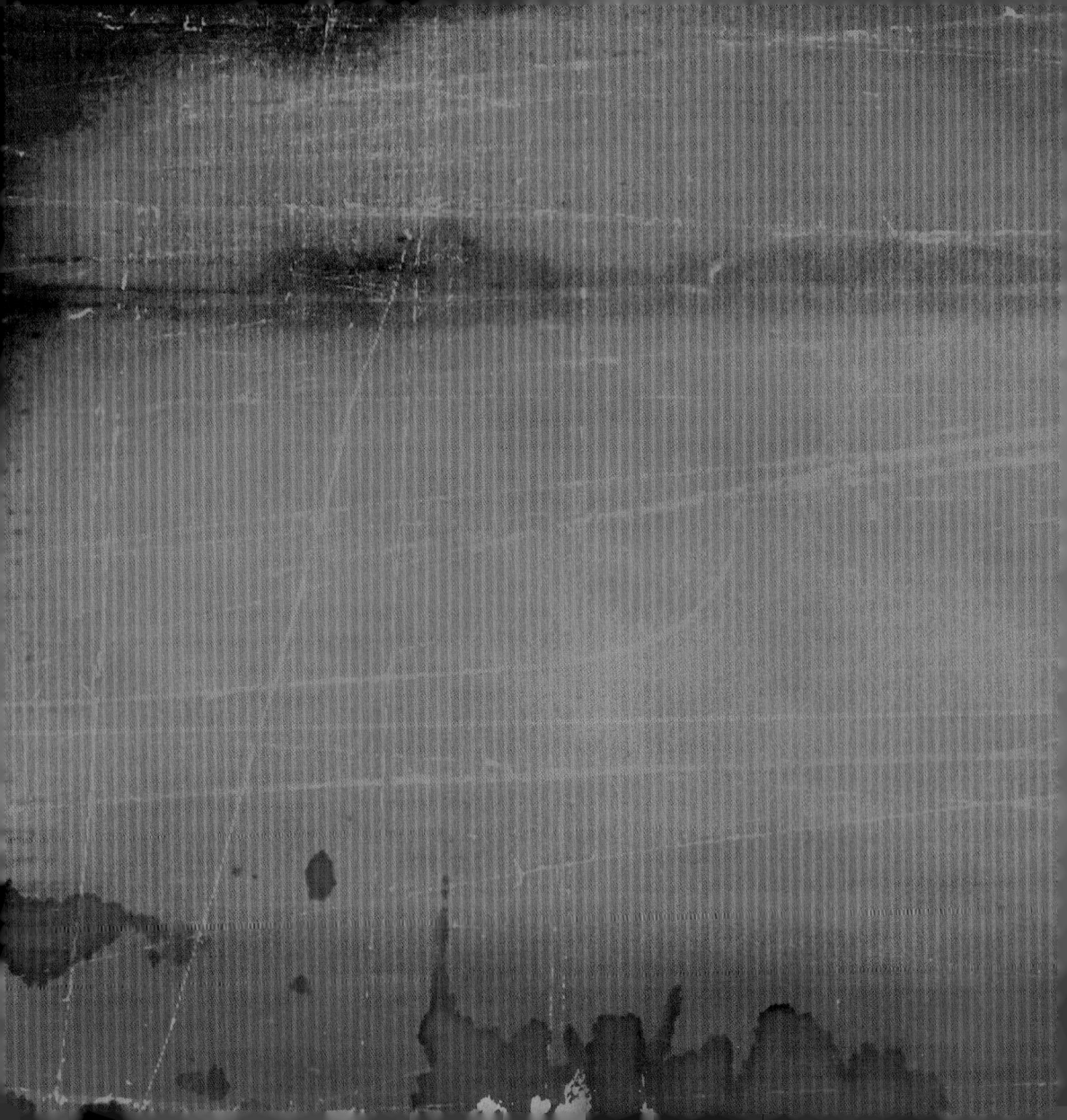

_____ TO

_____ FROM

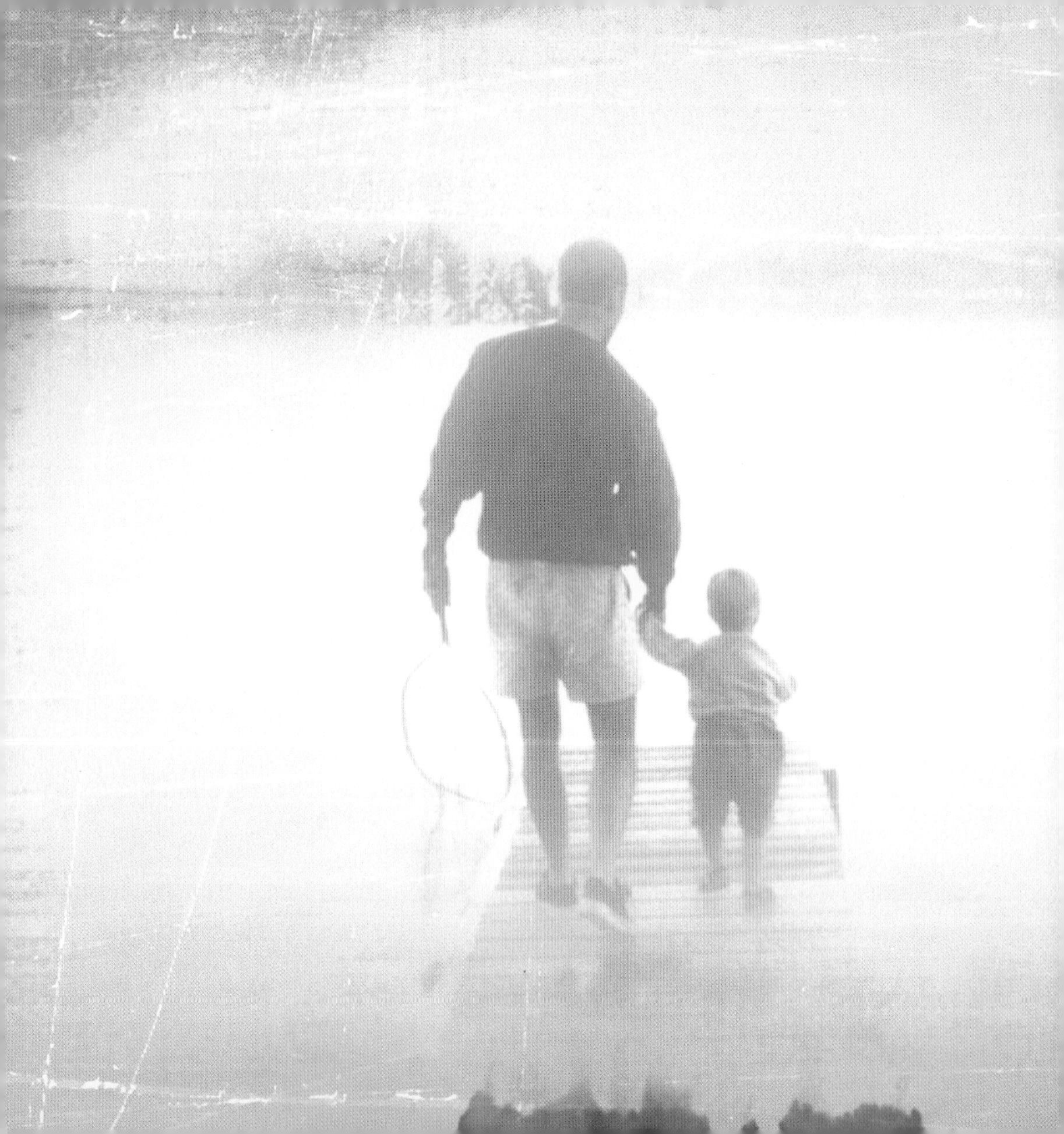

TO A CHILD LOVE IS SPELLED

t-i-m-e

*what a child **really needs** from you*

MAC ANDERSON & LANCE WUBBELS

simple truths®
Motivational & Inspirational Gifts

TO A CHILD LOVE IS SPELLED T·I·M·E

2004, 2006 by Mac Anderson and Koechel Peterson & Associates, Inc.
Cover and internal design © 2013 by Sourcebooks, Inc.

Sourcebooks, the colophon, and Simple Truths are registered trademarks of Sourcebooks, Inc.

All rights reserved. No part of this book may be reproduced in any form or by any electronic or mechanical means including information storage and retrieval systems—except in the case of brief quotations embodied in critical articles or reviews—without permission in writing from its publisher, Sourcebooks, Inc.

Cover and internal design by: Koechel Peterson & Associates, Inc. Minneapolis: MN

Published by Simple Truths, an imprint of Sourcebooks, Inc.
P.O. Box 4410, Naperville, Illinois 60567-4410
(630) 961-3900 : Fax: (630) 961-2168
www.sourcebooks.com

Printed and bound in China.

OGP 10 9 8 7 6 5 4 3 2

All that is worth cherishing in this world

begins in the heart, not in the head.

CONTENTS

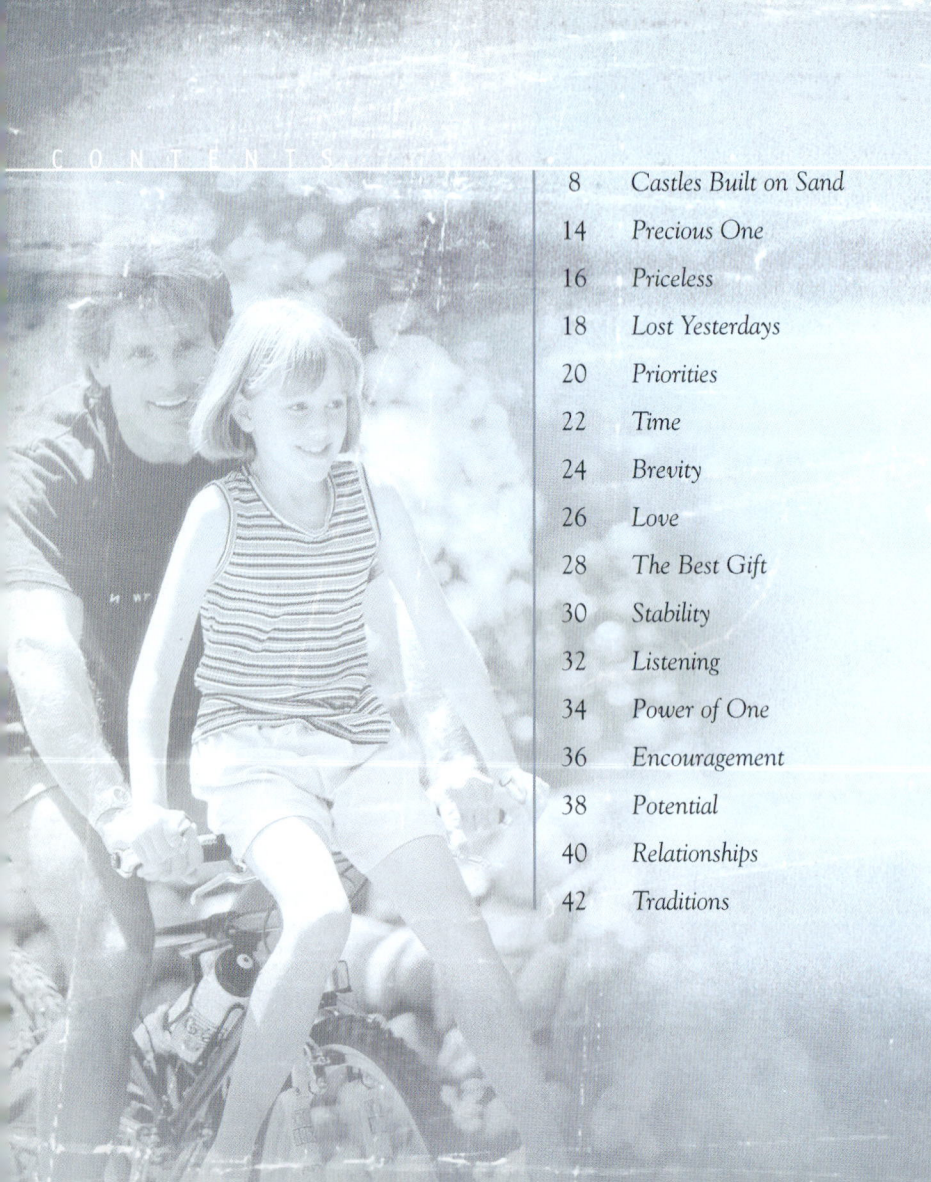

8	*Castles Built on Sand*
14	*Precious One*
16	*Priceless*
18	*Lost Yesterdays*
20	*Priorities*
22	*Time*
24	*Brevity*
26	*Love*
28	*The Best Gift*
30	*Stability*
32	*Listening*
34	*Power of One*
36	*Encouragement*
38	*Potential*
40	*Relationships*
42	*Traditions*

48	Values	82	Friends
50	Slow Down	84	First Things First
52	Possibilities	86	Entertainment
54	Choices	88	Letting Go
56	Strength	90	Surprises
58	Perseverance	92	Teach
60	Discipline	94	Support
62	The Greatest Gift	96	Delight
64	Responsibility	98	Understanding
66	Adversity	100	Passing the Torch
68	Moments	102	Roots
70	Mistakes	104	Attitude
72	Trust	106	Destiny
74	Faith	108	Keep Growing
76	The Measure of Success	110	About the authors
78	Focus		
80	Laughter		

CASTLES
BUILT ON SAND

IN THE FAINT LIGHT of the attic, an old man, tall and stooped, bent his great frame and made his way to a stack of boxes that sat near one of the little half-windows. Brushing aside a wisp of cobwebs, he tilted the top box toward the light and began to carefully lift out one old photograph album after another. Eyes once bright but now dim searched longingly for the source that had drawn him here.

It began with the fond recollection of the love of his life, long gone, and somewhere in these albums was a photo of her he hoped to rediscover. Silent as a mouse, he patiently opened the long buried treasures and soon was lost in a sea of memories. Although his world had not stopped spinning when his wife left it, the past was more alive in his heart than his present aloneness.

Setting aside one of the dusty albums, he pulled from the box what appeared to be a journal from his grown son's childhood. He could not recall ever having seen it before, or that his son had ever kept a journal. *Why did Elizabeth always save the children's old junk?* he wondered, shaking his white head.

Opening the yellowed pages, he glanced over a short reading, and his lips curved in an unconscious smile. Even his eyes brightened as he read the words that spoke clear and sweet to his soul. It was the voice of the little boy who had grown up far too fast in this very house, and whose voice had grown fainter and fainter over the years. In the utter silence of the attic, the words of a guileless six-year-old worked their magic and carried the old man back to a time almost totally forgotten.

Entry after entry stirred a sentimental hunger in his heart like the longing a gardener feels in the winter for the fragrance of spring flowers. But it was accompanied by the painful memory that his son's simple recollections of those days were far different from his own. But how different?

Reminded that he had kept a daily journal of his business activities over the years, he closed his son's journal and turned to leave, having forgotten the cherished photo that originally triggered his search. Hunched over to keep from bumping his head on the rafters, the old man stepped to the wooden stairway and made his descent, then headed down a carpeted stairway that led to the den.

Opening a glass cabinet door, he reached in and pulled out an old business journal. Turning, he sat down at his desk and placed the two journals beside each other. His was leather-bound and engraved neatly with his name in gold, while his son's was tattered and the name "Jimmy" had been nearly scuffed from its surface. He ran a long skinny finger over the letters, as though he could restore what had been worn away with time and use.

As he opened his journal, the old man's eyes fell upon an inscription that stood out because it was so brief in comparison to other days. In his own neat handwriting were these words:

Wasted the whole day fishing with Jimmy. Didn't catch a thing.

With a deep sigh and a shaking hand, he took Jimmy's journal and found the boy's entry for the same day, June 4. Large scrawling letters, pressed deeply into the paper, read:

Went fishing with my dad. Best day of my life.

PRECIOUS ONE

You get a knot in your throat

whenever you say the words.

"She's my little girl . . . always will be my little girl."

"He's my boy . . . my precious boy."

15

PRICELESS

You thought you knew

what love was

before your child got into your heart.

There is no limit,
    no measure,
        no end to this love.

You belong . . .
      literally . . . to each other.

That little girl is yours, and you are hers.
That boy is priceless . . . the joy of your soul.

*If we take care of the moments,
the years will take care of themselves.*

MARIA EDGEWORTH

LOST

But far too often we fail to realize there's a thief who works overtime to steal our time.

Precious moments with our children . . . where did they go? Lost minutes stretch into hours, then days. Lost yesterdays pass away and become weeks and months. We look back and shake our heads in disbelief, wondering where the years went.

YESTERDAYS

priorities

A hundred years from now, it will not matter

what my bank account was, the sort of house

I lived in, or the kind of car I drove.

But the world may be different because

I was important in the life of a child.

FOREST E. WITCRAFT

TIME

TIME IS THE RAW MATERIAL of your relationship with your child and must be guarded at all costs. It's true what they say: a bucket with a hole in it gets just as empty as a bucket that is deliberately kicked over. Life will shout a thousand demands to take you away from time spent with your child. If you permit the urgent to rule, you will lose time you can never recover or catch with your hand. What happens in the changing life of your child today will never be repeated. All the gold in the world cannot buy back either the little delights of the day or the big pleasures that happen without announcement or a plan. You simply have to be there.

*You will never find the time
    to spend with your children.
You have to make time and plan for it.
There is no other possible way.*

BREVITY

"Life is but a breath," so the Bible says.

So take a deep breath, fill your lungs, and think about it.

    Poof! and it's gone.

"My days are swifter than a runner, they fly away,"

    said the Old Testament patriarch Job.

And we can never catch them. We run out of breath.

Don't put your children off, even if you're tired.

Don't squelch the moment, even if it's inconvenient.

Nothing is more powerful than showing your love

    at the point of a felt need.

Tomorrow they may not be asking for you.

Life goes on, but children never stay the same.

LOVE

You can give without loving,
but you can never love without giving.

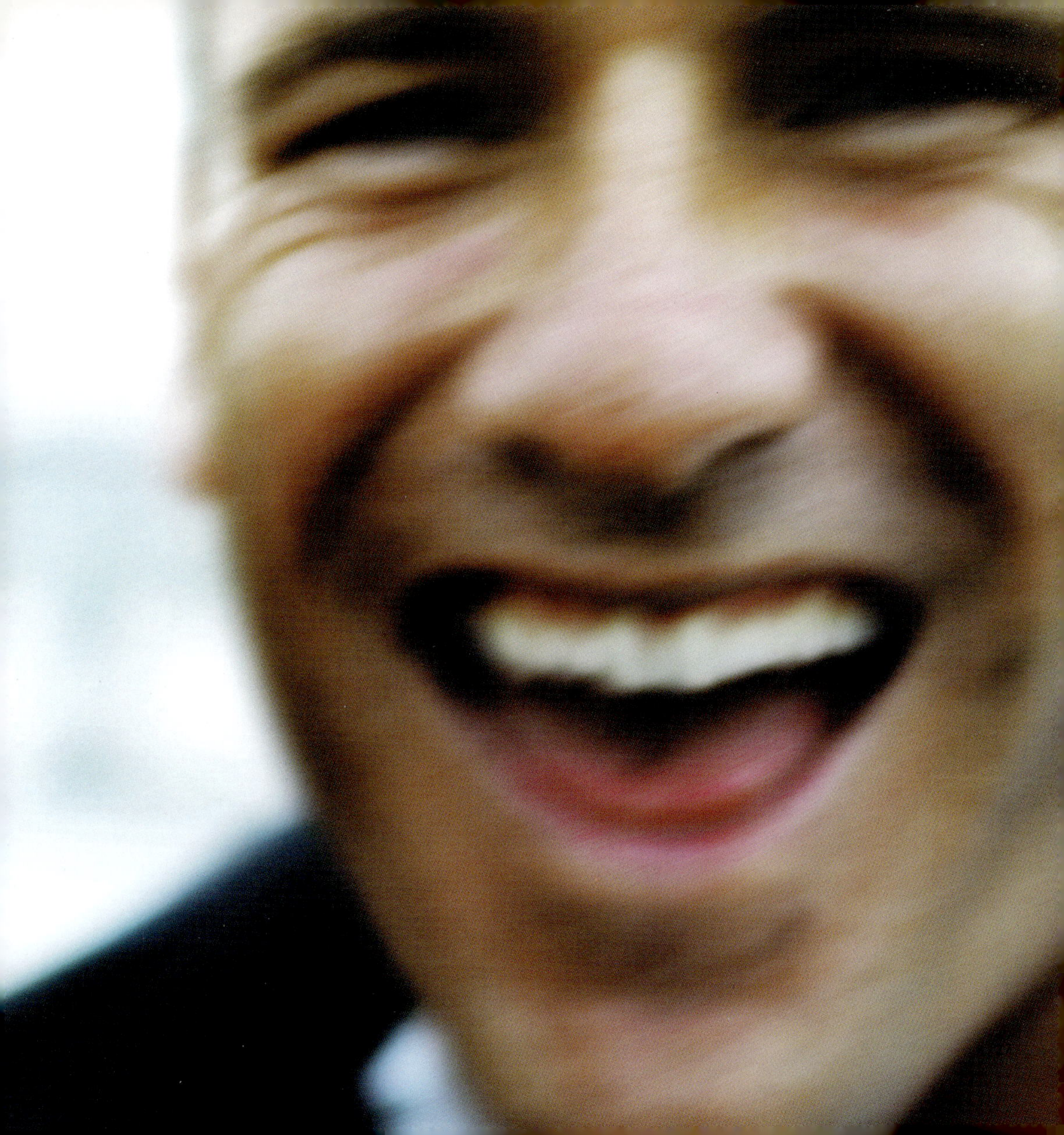

Time, indeed,
  is a sacred gift,
and each day is a little life.
JOHN LUBBOCK

THE BEST GIFT

NO AMOUNT OF LOVE is too much for any child, and you cannot separate love from time spent together. The fact that you feel love for your children does not guarantee that they feel loved. They need to constantly hear you tell them "I love you" and see your love demonstrated in the small details of life. Give your child the best gift of all—yourself. That's what they really want and need.

STABILITY

Your child's world is only as stable and safe as the life you provide. Children live in the present moment, not the past or the future, and you are the guide to the little universe they see and feel now. If your child is unsure of where you are, or what your mood might be at any given moment, or if you might leave, his world will be filled with constant turmoil. If you want her to grow up with confidence, it starts with what you bring with your life.

Children are what we make them.

FRENCH PROVERB

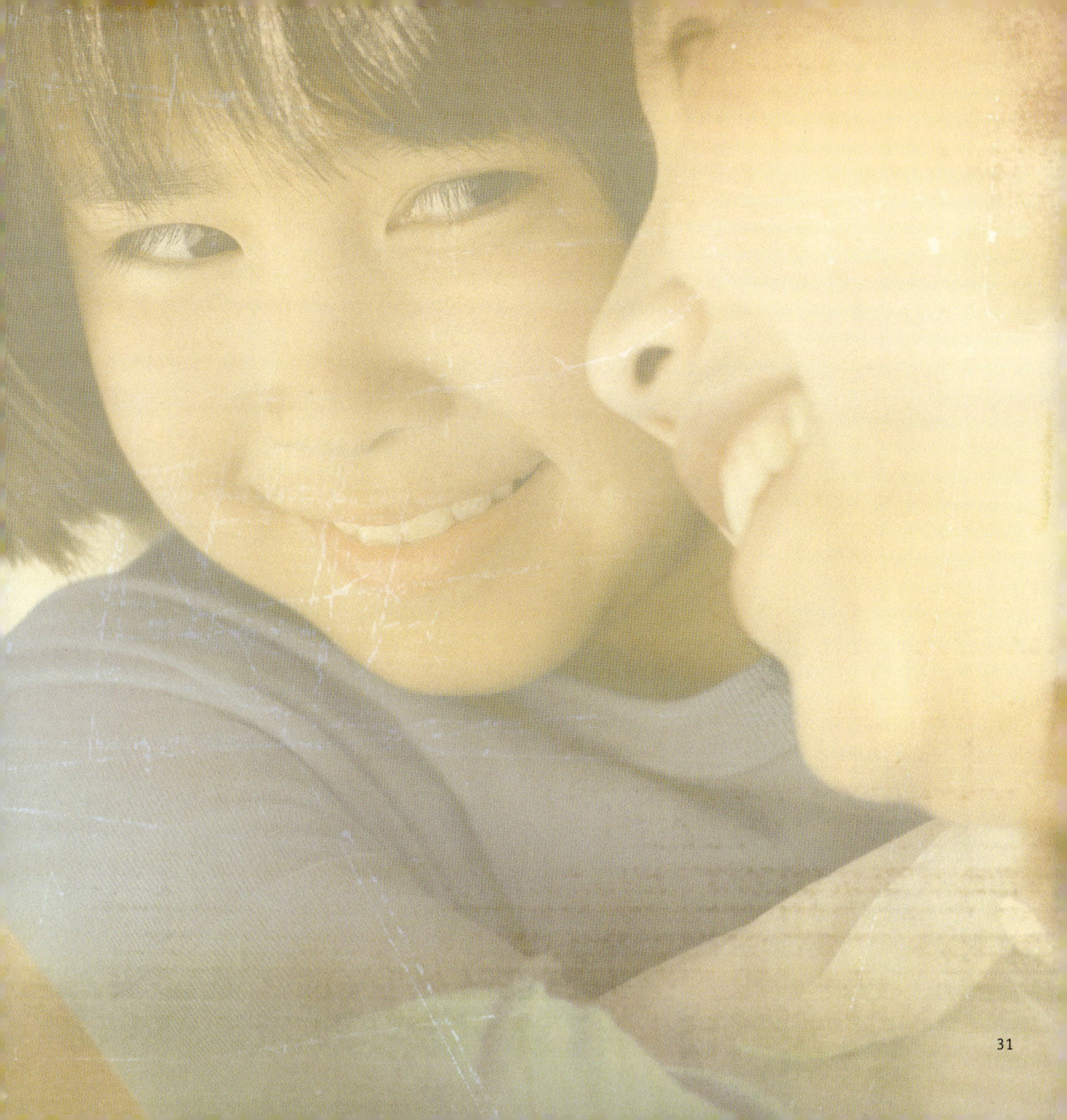

LISTENING

Seek first to understand, then to be understood.

YOU MUST TRAIN YOURSELF to listen for the whispers that come from your child's heart. Listening with the heart hears far more than spoken words. It picks up what's going on beneath the surface of a child's life. Do you know what your child fears by watching his body language? Can you sense her love in the way she squeezes your hand? Have you read his thoughts by the look in his eyes? In dozens of ways unique to your child, you must come to know your child without a word being spoken. Whether it's laughter or tears, silence or chatter, you know what he's really feeling. To hear the whispers beneath the surface, turn off the noise in your life and listen with your heart.

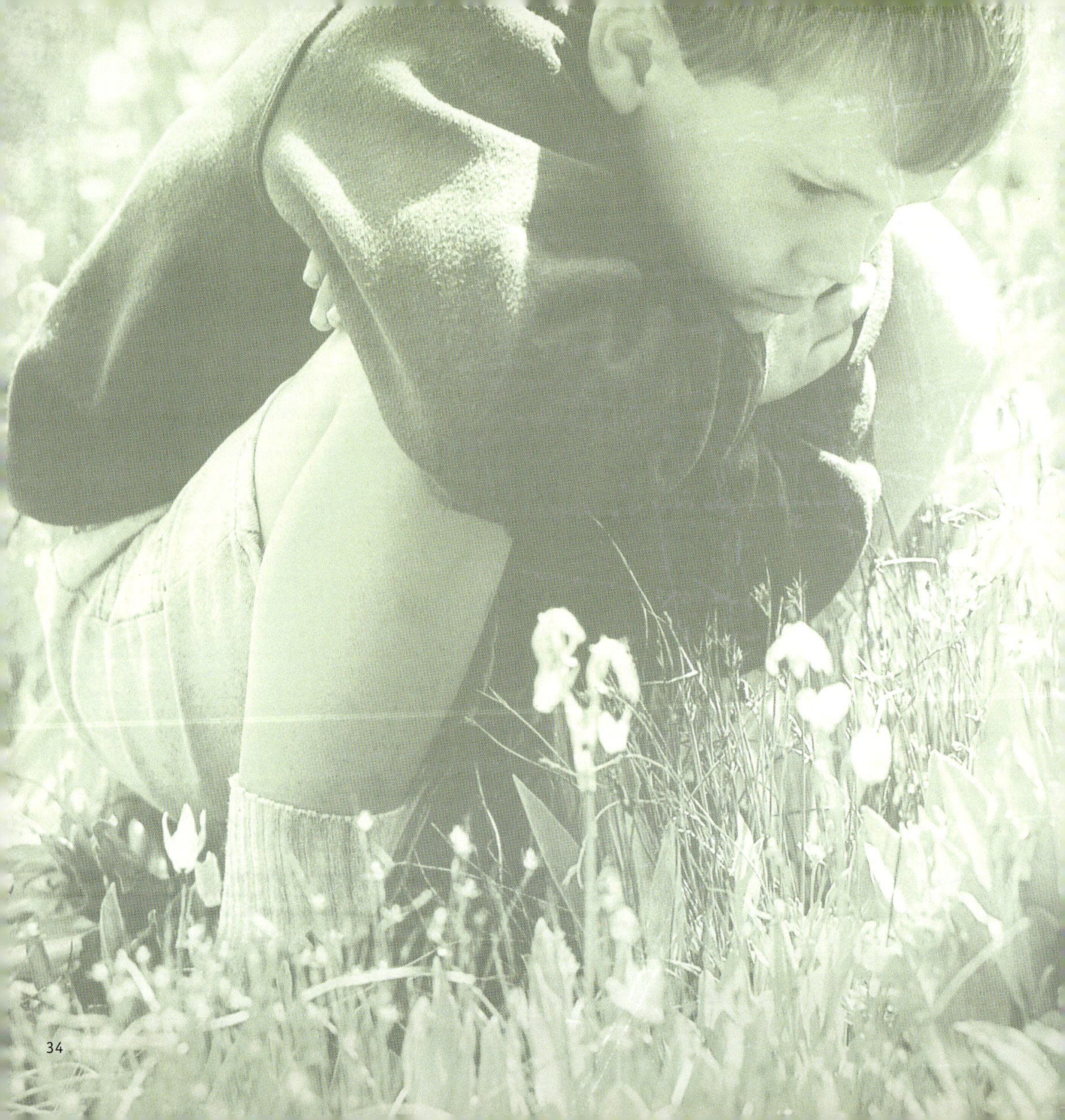

POWER OF ONE

TO THE WORLD,

    YOU MAY BE JUST ONE PERSON . . .

BUT TO ONE PERSON

    YOU MIGHT JUST BE THE WORLD.

ENCOURAGEMENT

Your son needs to know that you are his biggest fan in life. He needs you to claim him as your own, and for you to do it vocally. But he also needs to know that you will always be there to cheer, whether he "wins" or not. Your daughter needs to know that you see her as a winner because of who she is, not because she achieved something that earned your approval. It is crucial that your encouragement be as unconditional as your love. May your enthusiasm be as high when he falls down as when he scores the winning run. Never allow failures to diminish your support.

Encouragement

is oxygen to the soul.

GEORGE ADAMS

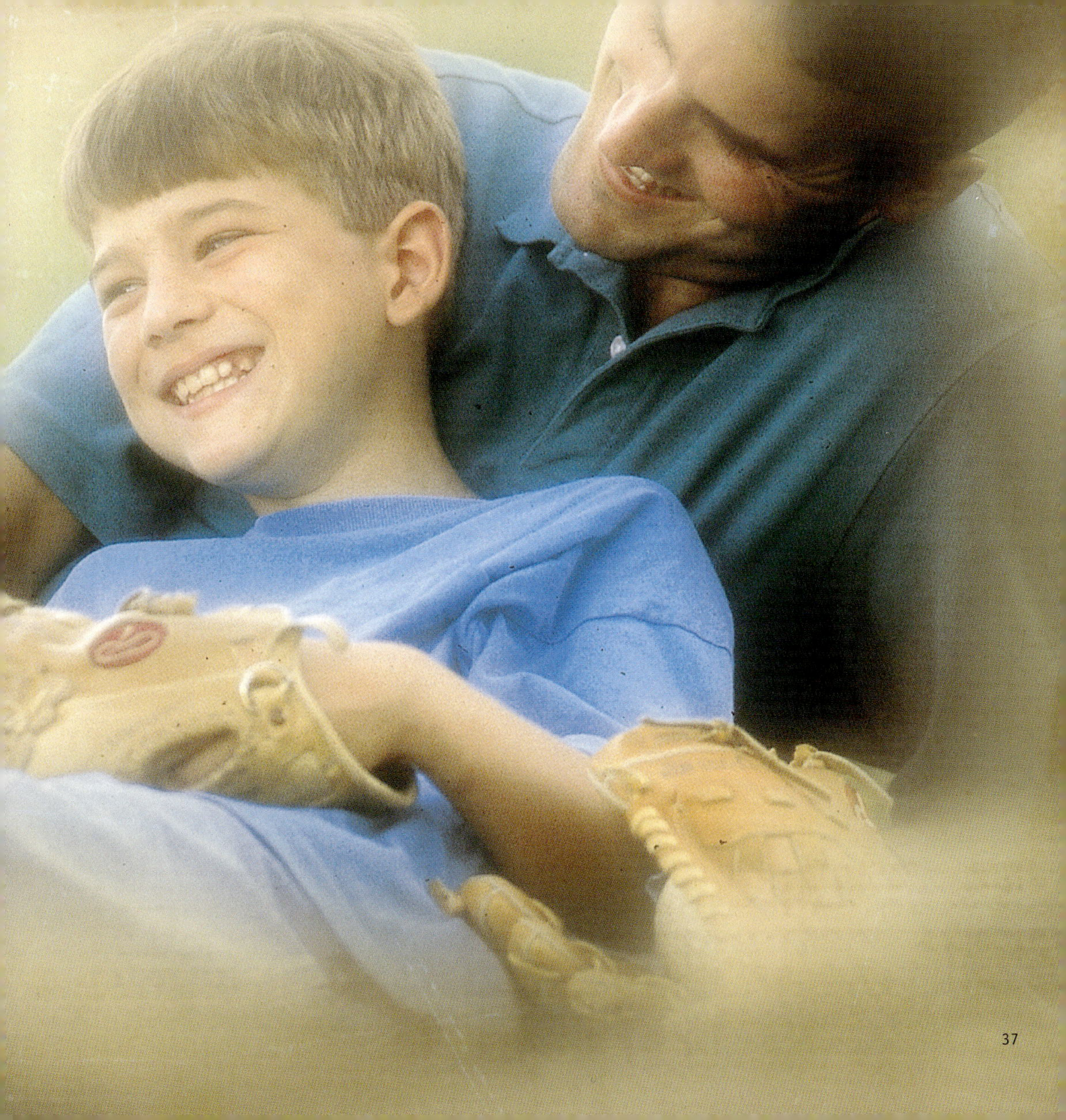

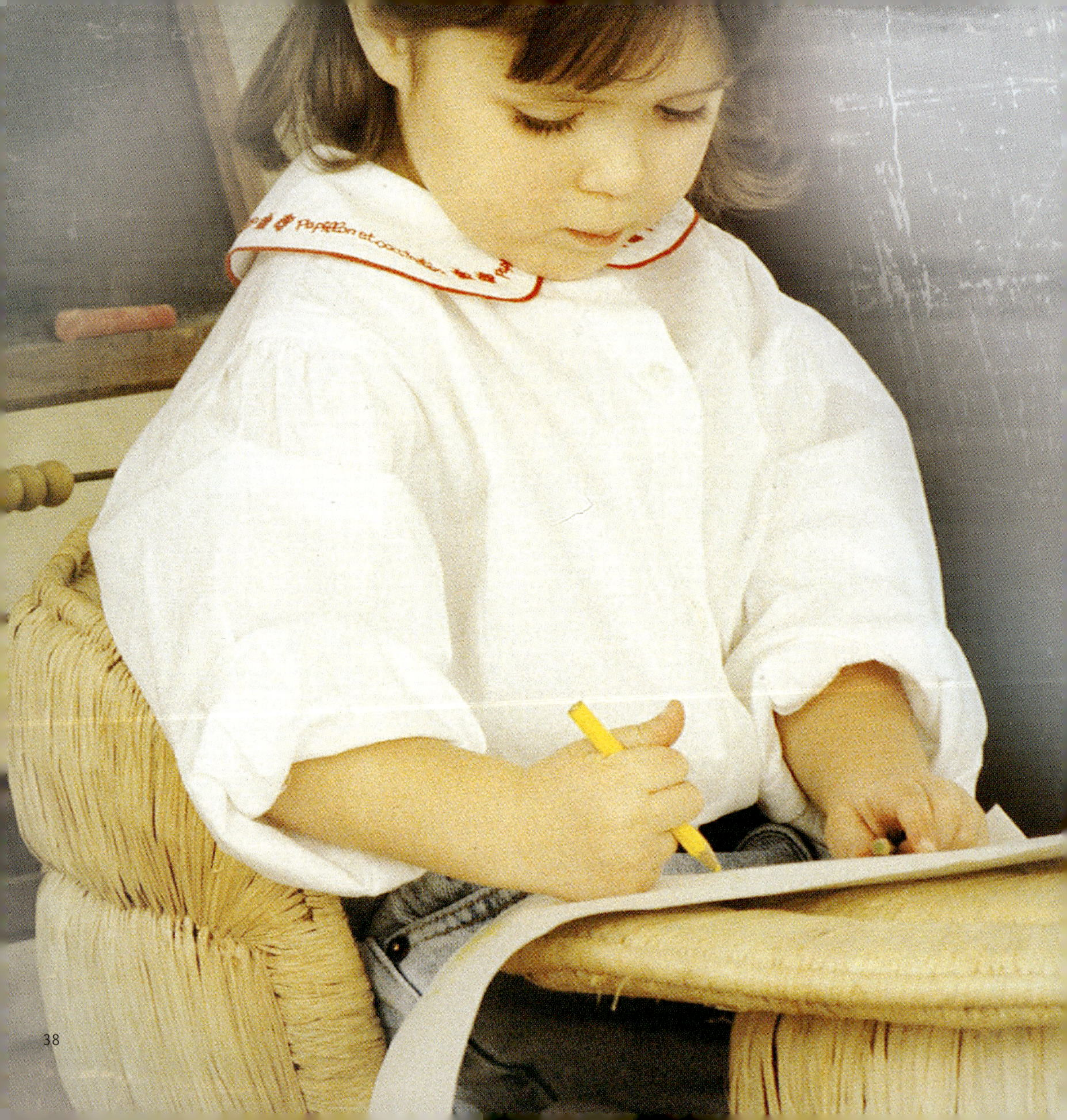

All children are artists, and it is an indictment of our culture that so many of them lose their creativity, their unfettered imaginations, as they grow older.

MADELEINE L'ENGLE

POTENTIAL

EVERY CHILD BEARS AN ORIGINALITY that is evidence of the Divine. How else do you explain your child's creativity and spontaneity and imagination? Who but the Creator could build in such a spirit of adventure and a curiosity to discover? God has filled your child with a magnificent potential that is distinct from any other person. And He has placed you as a parent to nurture and provide opportunities for your child to discover her interests and talents. Keep him warm in your love and enjoy the discovery with him. Delight in the way God has shaped her life and refuse to force her to perform as though all of life were an Olympic event.

RELATIONSHIPS

THE MOST IMPORTANT THINGS IN LIFE AREN'T THINGS.

TRADITIONS
TRADITIONS

It isn't the big pleasures

that count the most;

it is making a great deal

out of the little ones.

ANONYMOUS

When I (Lance) was a little boy, the arrivals of Easter and Christmas were always marked with an overwhelming sense of anticipation that ran deep through our small country home. As twilight deepened to darkness on the Saturday evening before Easter as well as on Christmas Eve, the buzz around the house was not about Easter eggs or Christmas presents, nor about the spiritual matters so deserving of our celebrating. No, the excitement was fixed on the fact that at any moment we would be receiving a personal visitation from the Easter Bunny or Santa Claus, depending upon the holiday.

The epiphany on the evening before Easter, for instance, always worked the same way . . . and never once failed to work its magic. As the darkness of the night set in, my sister and I would hear my mother suddenly call out from the kitchen, "Hey, what was that out there on the hill? Looks like a big rabbit hopping around." We would race to the kitchen and peer out the kitchen window into the looming black, and Mother would ask, "Do you see it?"

Then suddenly, from the living room, would come a tremendous banging on one of the windows. We would race out of the kitchen to try to catch a glimpse of the Easter Bunny's white paw at the window, but he was gone. Slowly, slowly, we would creep toward the darkened window where we thought the noise had come from, when the gigantic paw would bang another window where we weren't looking, and the explosion would drive us backward, often in a knee-buckling tumble, and always with screams of delight.

As soon as we had recovered and gathered our nerve, we would make a stealthy approach toward another window with hopes of discovering the elusive bunny, but that glimpse never came. He knew exactly where we were, and the knocks kept moving from room to room. The pandemonium would go on for perhaps ten minutes, and then the knocks would stop just as suddenly as they began. Moments later my father would come up from the basement, where he'd been working on a radio or something else, and was greeted with a dozen stories of all he had just missed.

Twenty years later, it was my opportunity to don the white gloves on the night before Easter and work the same Easter Bunny magic upon my little girl and boy. Though the years had passed, the thrill was the same. I raced around the house in the dark, banging on one window after another, while my kids screamed and howled and laughed and tumbled. If the snow was deep at Christmas, it slowed me down, but did not deter the delight of two children who will never forget those special moments.

That holiday tradition belongs to our family alone. I've never met another person who has had the Easter Bunny and Santa Claus personally bang on their windows. But I'll bet that when my children have children, that happy scene will be repeated again and again.

Here's the point. Laugh and play together. Create family traditions that are all your own, even if the neighbors look out their windows and think you've lost your mind as you race around your house pounding on windows in the dark. Our family traditions reminded me that we belonged to each other, that our family really was our family. No other family had the distinct honor or fun that our family had on these holidays.

Over the years these memories of intense joy rooted me to the past and became a source of strength. Traditions do not have to be expensive or elaborate or big. All you might need is a cheap white glove. But when the tradition becomes a part of who your child is as a person, the cost is of little matter.

THE GREATEST GIFTS MY PARENTS GAVE TO ME . . .

were their unconditional love and set of values.

Values that they lived and didn't just lecture about.

Values that included an understanding of the simple difference

between right and wrong,

a belief in God,

the importance of hard work and education,

self-respect and a belief in America.

COLIN POWELL

VALUES

slow down

Train yourself to slow down, for your children's sake . . . if not for your own. Have you noticed that he won't talk with you when you have more "important" things to do?

Stop the hurried pace and take a good look into her eyes. Relax and let the world keep on spinning without your help for a while. Talk and listen . . . patiently. Be quiet and let your son bring you into his world. Duct tape your mouth shut if you must. When you speak, make yourself transparent and unguarded. Invite your daughter into your world by expressing how you felt when you were a child. Share your memories. Remember: The opportunity may not come often . . .

OR EVER.

Our greatest danger in life

is in permitting the urgent things

to crowd out the important.

CHARLES E. HUMMEL

POSSIBILITIES

Are you a student of your child and their world? If not, your child needs you to become one—fast! Do you know the boundless imagination, the bright hopes, and the silent wonder that roam about in his heart? Can you sense the changing seasons in her life, some filled with mystery and beauty and others fraught with disappointment and heartbreak? A wide ocean of possibilities lies before your child, but there is nothing simple about the journey to adulthood. Will you be there to guide and protect your child from the dangers along the way? It all begins with knowing your child.

How beautiful is youth!
How bright it gleams with its illusions,
aspirations, dreams! Book of Beginnings,
Story without End. Each maid a heroine,
and each man a friend.

HENRY WADSWORTH LONGFELLOW

Things that matter most
must never be
at the mercy
of things
that matter least.

GOETHE

CHOICES

STRENGTH

The heart of a child is amazingly delicate, yet wonderfully resilient. You touch a child's soul profoundly with the simple words "I love you." And when you put your arms around your child as only you can, it is even more meaningful. The most powerful way to show love to your child is to show love to your spouse. It is in keeping your marriage strong that you meet your child's needs for love. The Chinese have a proverb that speaks to families: "In a broken nest there are few whole eggs." Tough love will keep your nest from breaking.

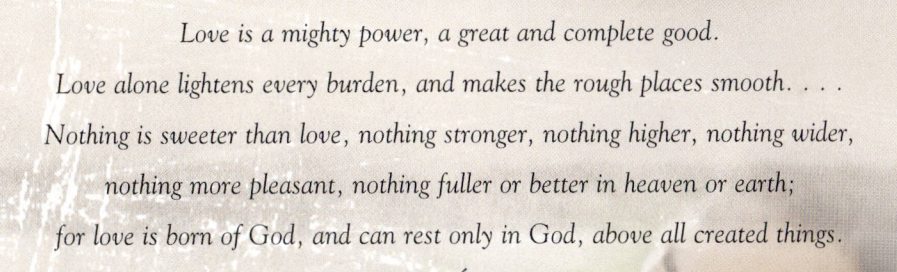

Love is a mighty power, a great and complete good.
Love alone lightens every burden, and makes the rough places smooth. . . .
Nothing is sweeter than love, nothing stronger, nothing higher, nothing wider,
nothing more pleasant, nothing fuller or better in heaven or earth;
for love is born of God, and can rest only in God, above all created things.

THOMAS Á KEMPIS

*The great man is he
who does not lose
his child's heart.*

MENCIUS

PERSEVERANCE

You may be tested to the limits, but never allow the lines of communication to be cut between you and your child. Isolation sabotages any relationship, and you can't let that happen with your child. If she stops talking, be patient and keep talking. Keep the doors open and don't give up when you feel as though you're talking to a brick wall. Holding back your love when you're frustrated will not solve anything. Loving strength and support will make an impact, even when you think it won't. How you respond to difficult times will influence whether the test turns into a pattern in your child's life.

DISCIPLINE

THE SECRET TO ALL CHILD training and discipline is l-o-v-e. The focus should not be on the rules you set but on your relationship. Children flourish in an environment where they are given strong direction that allows them to move safely toward personal independence. Be deliberate about setting rules that are realistic and clearly understood, then be consistent in your discipline. Keep in mind that the goal of the discipline is to shape your child's character and values, and obedience and respect are at the heart of it. It's not about punishing your child; it's about effecting positive change in his or her life. And it only happens in the context of a loving relationship.

Call them rules or call them limits,
good ones, I believe, have this in common:
    they serve reasonable purposes;
        they are practical and within
a child's capability; they are consistent;
and they are an expression
of loving concern.

FRED ROGERS

f you leave your child
ith a positive attitude,
ou leave them
of incalculable value.

THE GREATEST GIFT

If you leave your child

with a positive attitude,

you leave them

an estate of incalculable value.

At every step the child should be allowed to meet the real experiences of life; the thorns should never be plucked from his roses.
ELLEN KEY

RESPONSIBILITY

IT IS OFTEN AN UNPLEASANT EXPERIENCE for a parent, but a child must be allowed to experience the consequences for his actions and decisions. Whenever you intervene, you rob him of taking personal responsibility for his life, and you hinder the shaping of his personality. It is only when we face the consequences of our actions that we learn to change our behavior and do the right thing. Before you step in and get involved, consider whether the consequences of your child's actions will be harmful to his person. If not, let the chips fall as one of life's little instructive hard knocks goes to work.

LIFE IS FULL OF ADVERSITY... and times of failure. Your children need you to show them how to face challenges and the unexpected with courage, and how to use their failures as opportunities to learn and grow. Don't circumvent the process and bail them out. Tell them about the challenges and failures of your life, and how you've gotten through them. Show them how to refuse to stay down when they get knocked down, and that to begin again is the first step to success.

ADVERSITY

Success is never final.
Failure is never fatal.
It's courage that counts.
JOHN WOODEN

IT IS NOT THE DAYS

BUT MOMENTS

that will capture your heart forever.

MISTAKES

Teach your children . . .

through your own experiences . . .

that failures do not harm them

    unless they start excusing them or they stop trying.

AS A PARENT WE MAKE MISTAKES, AND WE KNOW IT, AND OUR CHILDREN CERTAINLY KNOW IT.

The fact that you're not perfect is not the problem. The problem comes when we refuse to admit our mistakes, or even try to justify them. Admitting our mistake and asking for forgiveness if we have hurt our child teaches honesty and keeps the doors of communication open. And if it is followed by true change in your behavior, your child will see the change in your life that will set the standard for his life. If you want his respect and love, it starts with how you respond to your own mistakes.

YOUR CHILDREN NEED you to teach them the value of trust. If they lie, deceive, or disobey, show them how deeply it damages your relationship and restricts the amount of freedom you can give them. But teaching the importance of trust begins with the model you set before them. If your own words cannot be trusted, however small and insignificant the words may seem at the time, don't expect your children to practice telling the truth. If you break promises you make to your child, expect her to do the same. And guard her privacy and keep personal secrets to yourself. Trust must reign as king in your home.

It's frightening to think that you mark your child merely by being yourself.

SIMONE de BEAUVOIR

73

Be careful what you put . . .

    or allow others to put . . .

        into your child's heart.

It will stay there forever.

FAITH

YOUR CHILDREN DEPEND UPON YOU to provide them with a system of values to live by—basic beliefs about right and wrong. Faith is a core value we need to share with them. What we believe about God and His Son Jesus Christ and the Bible and eternal life needs to be imparted to them. But as is true of all values, our faith must be real if we want our children to imitate it. Values are learned from examples in daily life, and if our lives contradict what we say we believe, our children will see through the hypocrisy and reject it. Don't underestimate the power of a genuine spiritual life.

THE MEASURE OF SUCCESS

*The measure of real success
is one you cannot spend . . .
it's the way your child
describes you when
speaking to a friend.*

THE ONLY WAY YOU ARE GOING TO KNOW what is going on in your child's life is to give him your undivided time. Stop what you're doing and really be there. Turn off the television and stereos and sit down together. Give your son the freedom to talk, encourage him to express himself, and he will feel loved and important. When you do, you'll discover what he's facing. Focus on your daughter's needs, and you'll get a clear picture of her heart. Don't leave love to chance.

A child's life is like a piece of paper

on which every person

leaves a mark.

CHINESE PROVERB

FOCUS

LAUGHTER

Kitchens are made for long talks and close friends,

loving families and lots of laughter.

Kitchens are made for daydreams

and growing things and creative moments,

for sharing and preparing the blessings of life.

ANONYMOUS

Do not be misled:

"Bad company corrupts good character."

1 CORINTHIANS 15:33 NIV

FRIENDS

CELEBRATE THE FRIENDSHIPS that have a positive influence in your child's life, and turn your home into a place where your child's friends like to gather and play. Make a difference by doing all you can to stay involved. You need to know whom your child is spending his time with, what they do when they're together, and where they are. Show your child that the wrong friends can leave scars. And make sure they know the difference between being used and being accepted. Never surrender your child to the negative influences from certain friends.

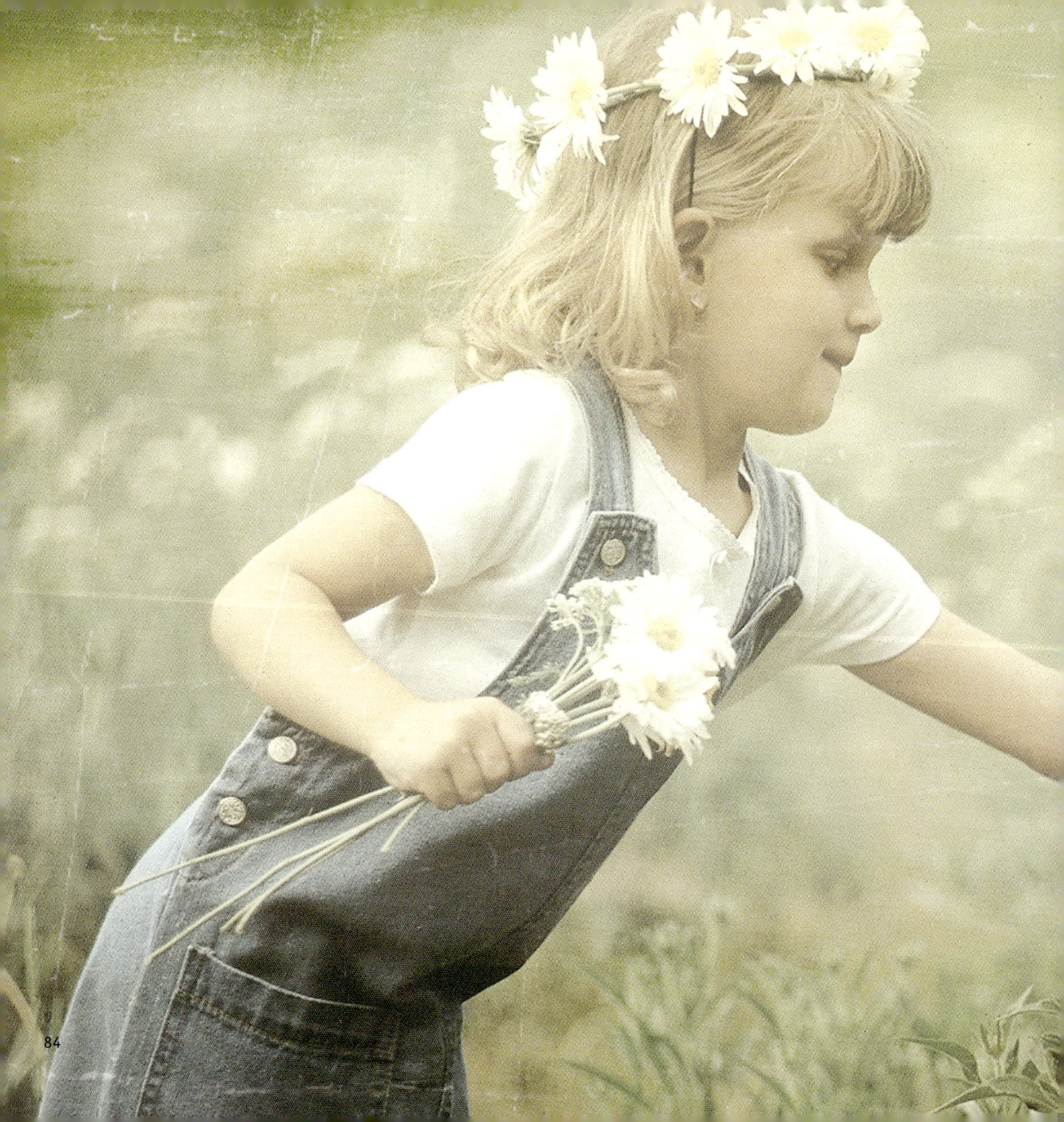

FIRST THINGS FIRST

Play is the work of childhood.

ENTERTAINMENT

Hollywood is a place where they'll pay you $10,000 for a kiss and fifty cents for your soul.

MARILYN MONROE

DON'T LET HOLLYWOOD take an obsessive role in your child's life. Television and movies have become the teachers of modern morality and will fill your child's mind with megadoses of illusions about real life, if you let them. Much of today's music and MTV offer a seductive influence that is killing the innocence of our children. And the Internet has a dark side that often creeps into the intimacy of our homes with the click of a mouse behind closed doors. Your child needs you to monitor every form of entertainment that influences them and to teach them to be media savvy. Fill their time with good things, and show them that joy comes from participating in life, not from illusions.

LETTING GO

There are two lasting bequests

we can give our children:

one is roots,

the other is wings.

HODDING CARTER

YOU FELT THE KNOT in your stomach the first time your child took off on a bicycle without your help, riding with the wind and laughing with delight. Your heart throbbed when the big yellow bus loomed down your street, and you kissed your little one good-bye. Every wave that follows takes your child farther from you. We feel the pain of letting go from the day our child is born. But as hard as it is, we have to allow our child to grow wings and eventually fly away. Mistakes will be made, you'll have to loosen the controls, and finding a balance is never easy. Each stage of a child's life brings new challenges . . . and new joys.

SURPRISES

A child can never be better than what his parents think of him.
MARCELENE COX

Leave notes for your children and you'll be surprised by their reactions. It only takes a few seconds to write "You're the love of my life" and drop it in her shoe, but it may never be forgotten. A note stuck to your son's jacket, telling him how glad you are to be his father, may be the boost he needs to get through a difficult day in school. A handwritten letter sent to your daughter may reach her heart in a way that all the talking in the world can't dent. It's an easy way to remind your child that you love them and are always thinking about them.

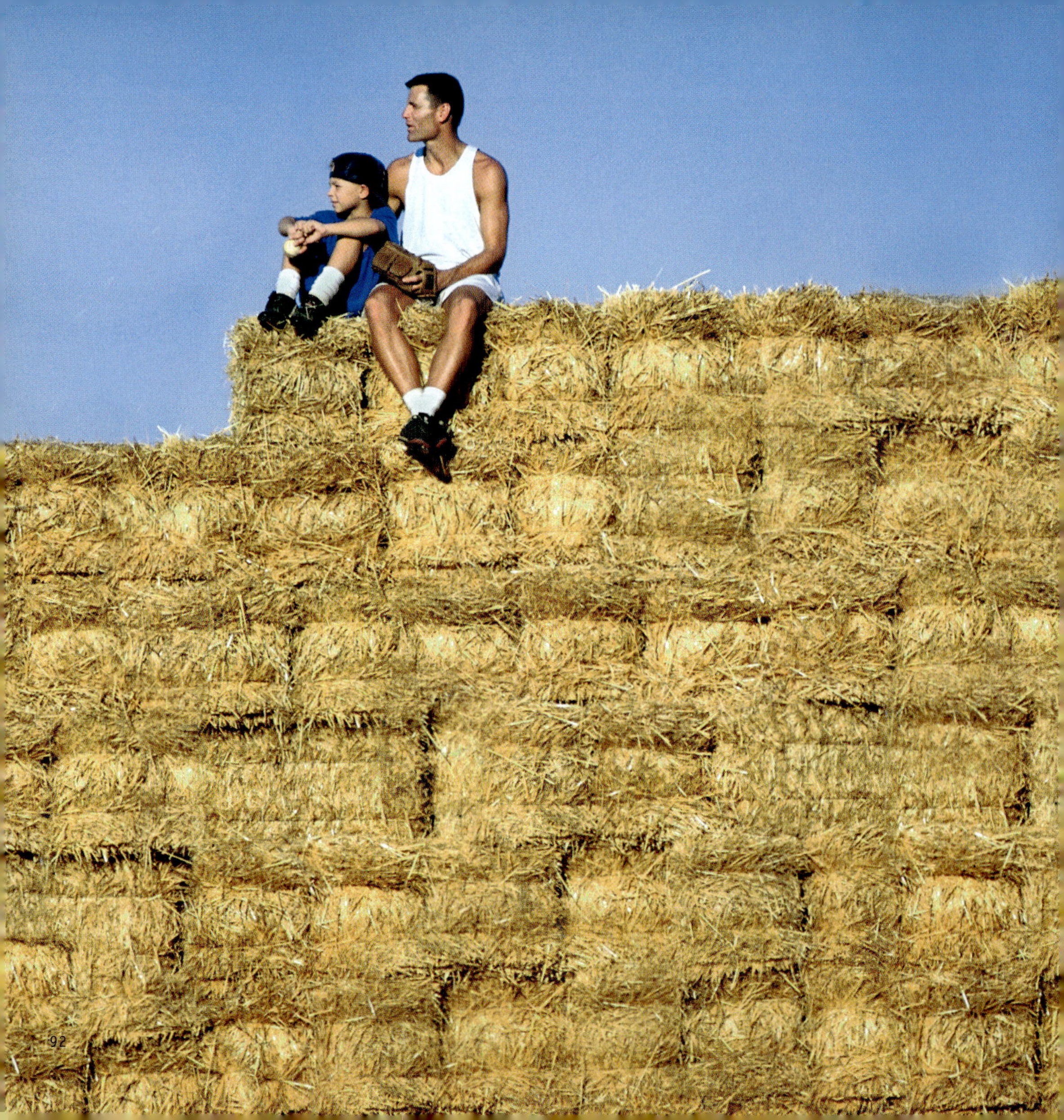

If it is to be . . . it's up to me.

T E A C H

THERE WILL COME TIMES when your children need you to cover them with your wings and protect them from life's storms. You'll sense it intuitively in your spirit, and these are moments you can't afford to not be there. Your children need to know that you are committed to standing beside them and helping them through the rough places of their lives. They need your strength to help them learn to persevere through difficulties and turmoil. Be there for them when it's tough, and they'll never forget that you were the one who helped them make their way to the other side.

s u p p o r t

Allow your child
to lean on you
and to keep from stumbling.

DELIGHT

A rich child often sits

    in a poor mother's lap.

DANISH PROVERB

ENJOY YOUR CHILDREN, delight in them, and they will take pleasure in you. You'll never find a hand that feels so good as your child's. Nothing in this creation compares to cuddling and snuggling with your little one. Have you searched the fathoms of the mystery in your child's eyes? Have you listened to your child's prayers and cried out to God for such a simple faith? Do you delight in holding your precious one in the night, even till morning's light? If you miss the joy of being a parent, your child will miss the fullness of your love.

UNDERSTANDING

BEWARE OF TURNING MOLEHILLS of frustration with your child into mountains of separation. Beware of blowing issues all out of proportion and turning them into painful crises. Strive to put yourself in your child's shoes and feel what he feels. That doesn't mean you agree with him or that a "no" or a specific discipline is not needed. But it means you first listen and understand before you react. And it means you'll walk in love when you feel the least like loving.

*Start every day
  with your child
  as a new day,
a new beginning
  filled with fresh
  opportunities.*

PASSING THE TORCH

Children are living messages

we send to a time we will not see.

ROOTS

GIVE YOUR CHILDREN THE GIFT of roots by telling them your family's stories, whether you feel like a storyteller or not. The point is not so much to entertain as to enrich your child's life with a sense of belonging to you and to your parents and your grandparents. You are the one who can make uncles and aunts and cousins come alive for your child. To belong, to be able to say this is my family, brings a sense of value, a sense of something to be protected and valued. That's a good thing, but it will be missed if those stories remain untold.

What gift has Providence bestowed on man that is so dear to him as children?

CICERO

ATTITUDE

Teach your child that a positive attitude is a powerful force that will move him in the right direction even when life's winds are pushing him backward. Remind him that though we cannot change the winds, we can grow strong when we refuse to give up. Praise your child's positive attitudes and achievements and good behavior. Encourage him whenever he tries to do something beyond what he's already done. Reward him with appropriate gifts, such as lots of hugs.

Nothing can stop the man
  with the right mental attitude . . .
nothing on earth can help the man
  with the wrong mental attitude.
THOMAS JEFFERSON

DESTINY

*Teach a child
to choose the right path,
and when he is older
he will remain upon it.*

PROVERBS 22:6 THE LIVING BIBLE

KEEP GROWING

A truly rich man
   is one whose children
run into his arms.

YOU HAVE NEVER FACED A CHALLENGE BIGGER than parenting, and perhaps now that you're at the end of the book, you feel it's bigger than ever. You came into parenthood underequipped for the role, and you'll probably never feel you're up to the task. If you're really fortunate, you'll realize that being a good parent is something you're always becoming…as long as you're willing to grow and keep loving. It's not about the changes you force into your child's life but by the changes you allow God to make in you. This is true whether you're twenty or seventy. So relax, keep praying for your child and asking God for wisdom. Love is one investment that will never fail you.

ABOUT THE AUTHORS

MAC ANDERSON is the founder of Simple Truths and Successories, Inc., the leader in designing and marketing products for motivation and recognition. These companies, however, are not the first success stories for Mac. He was also the founder and CEO of McCord Travel, the largest travel company in the Midwest, and part owner/VP of sales and marketing for Orval Kent Food Company, the country's largest manufacturer of prepared salads.

His accomplishments in these unrelated industries provide some insight into his passion and leadership skills. He also brings the same passion to his speaking where he speaks to many corporate audiences on a variety of topics, including leadership, motivation, and team building.

Mac has authored or co-authored thirteen books that have sold over three million copies. His titles include: *Change Is Good…You Go First, Charging the Human Battery, Customer Love, Finding Joy, Learning to Dance in the Rain, 212°: The Extra Degree, Motivational Quotes, The Nature of Success, The Power of Attitude, The Essence of Leadership, The Dash,* and *You Can't Send a Duck to Eagle School*

For more information about Mac, visit www.simpletruths.com

LANCE WUBBELS is presently the vice president of literary development at Koechel Peterson & Associates, Inc., in Minneapolis, Minnesota. For the previous eighteen years, Wubbels worked as the managing editor of Bethany House Publishers as well as a teacher at Bethany College of Missions in Bloomington, Minnesota.

He is the author of *I Wish for You, Dance While You Can, If Only I Knew* with Hallmark Books, and *Bible Nobodies Who Became Somebodies* with Destiny Image. He has published seven fiction books with Bethany House Publishers and won an Angel Award for his novel, *One Small Miracle*. He has also compiled and edited twenty-five Christian Living Classic books published by Emerald Books. His daily devotional, *In His Presence*, won the 1999 Gold Medallion Award from the Evangelical Christian Publishers Association.

simple truths®
Motivational & Inspirational Gifts

To share how this book has encouraged you or someone close to you, send us an email at: customercare@simpletruths.com

To read more heartfelt stories, view life-inspiring movies, enjoy daily devotionals, quotes and Scriptures to strengthen and inspire your faith—and to share with a friend—visit us at www.simpletruths.com

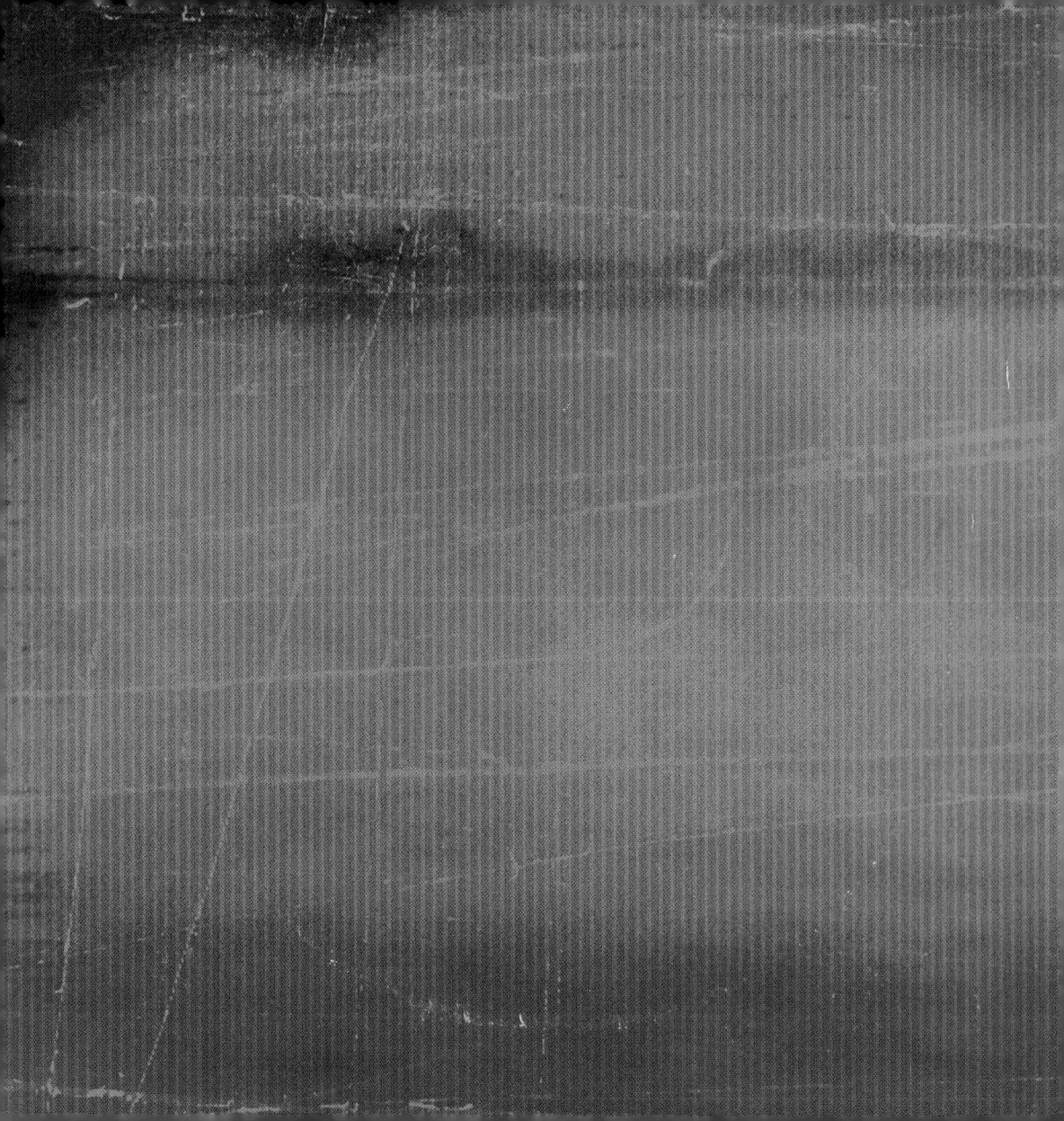